MW01101118

Canada's Political Parties

THE
GREEN PARTY

Gillian Poulter

Weigl

Published by Weigl Educational Publishers Limited
6325 10th Street SE
Calgary, Alberta
T2H 2Z9

Website: www.weigl.ca

Library and Archives Canada Cataloguing in Publication Data

Poulter, Gillian, 1952-
        Green Party / Gillian Poulter.

(Canada's political parties)
Includes index.
ISBN 978-1-77071-696-4 (bound)--ISBN 978-1-77071-701-5 (pbk.)

        1. Green Party of Canada. I. Title. II. Series: Canada's
political parties (Calgary, Alta.)

JL197.G74P68 2011   j324.271'0987   C2011-900816-5

Printed in the United States of America in North Mankato, Minnesota
1 2 3 4 5 6 7 8 9 0 15 14 13 12 11

072011
WEP040711

Project Coordinator: Heather Kissock
Design: Terry Paulhus

Photograph Credits
CP Images: pages 6B, 10, 11BL, 11BR, 12, 16, 18, 20, 21BL, 21BR, 24M; Dreamstime: page 4; Getty
Images: pages 8, 9, 11TL, 11TR, 13, 14, 15, 17, 19, 21TL, 24TL, 24TR, 24TM, 24B, 25TL, 25BL, 25BR, 26,
27; Green Party of Canada: pages 7B, 21TR, 25M; iStockphoto: page 25TR; Trevor Hancock: page 6T.

Every reasonable effort has been made to trace ownership and to obtain permission to reprint copyright
material. The publishers would be pleased to have any errors or omissions brought to their attention so
that they may be corrected in subsequent printings.

We acknowledge the financial support of the Government of Canada through the Canada Book Fund for
our publishing activities.

CONTENTS

Overview of Canada's Political Parties

Political parties in Canada are made up of people with similar beliefs who have joined together to accomplish specific goals. To achieve these goals, the party attempts to elect enough members to gain control of the government.

Political parties are central to our political system. In their attempts to win elections, parties propose a series of social, economic, and political policies called the party platform. The election campaign then attempts to convince the people to vote for candidates who support these beliefs. This process provides the people with a way of expressing their opinions and of holding the winning party accountable for its actions.

Beginnings

The first Canadian political parties started in central Canada in the 1820s and 1830s. They were created to ensure that the people's wishes were presented to the British governor who ruled the **colonies**. The achievement of **responsible government** in the late 1840s paved the way for the emergence of party politics as we know it today. When Canada became a nation in 1867, there was only the Liberal Party and the Conservative Party. These two parties dominated politics until the 1920s. The rise of the Progressive Party in the 1920s, and the emergence of the Co-operative Commonwealth Federation and the Social Credit parties in the 1930s gave voters more choices through which to express their concerns. However, these "third" parties never seriously challenged the power of the two major parties.

This situation changed, however, in the 1980s. The Reform Party began in 1987 as an alternative to the Progressive Conservative Party. In 2000, it transformed into the Canadian Alliance, which then merged with the Progressive Conservative Party in 2003 to form the Conservative Party of Canada. Today, the Conservative Party, Liberal Party, New Democratic Party (NDP), Green Party, and Bloc Québécois compete to dominate Canadian politics.

The Parliament Buildings in Ottawa have been the centre of Canadian politics since 1867.

The Green Party—
Its Beliefs and Philosophy

Although it now has policies on a wide range of social, political, and economic issues, Canada's Green Party has the same basic objectives as Green parties around the world. These objectives are to use political means to protect and improve the environment and promote **social justice.**

Green Values

The Green Party of Canada shares the six key values expressed in the Charter of the Global Greens. This is a document created in 2001 that details the guiding principles of Green parties across the globe. Canada's Green Party bases its platform on the following core values of the Charter.

- Ecological Wisdom: Acknowledgement that human beings are part of the natural world and respect for the specific values of all forms of life

- Non-Violence: A commitment to non-violence and a culture of peace and cooperation between nations

- Social Justice: Support for the fair distribution of resources to ensure that all have full opportunities for personal and social development

- Sustainability: Recognition of the scope for the material expansion of society within the **biosphere**, and the need to maintain **biodiversity** through the use of **renewable resources**

- Participatory **Democracy**: Attainment of a democracy in which all citizens have the right to express their views and are able to directly participate in decisions which affect their lives

- Respect for Diversity: Honour equally the Earth's biological and ecological diversity together with the context of individual responsibility toward all beings

Registering a Political Party

1. Political parties do not have to be registered with the government. However, registered parties can provide tax receipts for donations, thus saving the donors money. An official party can place its name beneath its candidates' names on the ballot.

2. To be registered, a party must:
- Have statements from at least 250 individuals who are qualified to vote (i.e. 18 years old and a Canadian citizen) indicating that they are party members
- Endorse (sponsor) at least one candidate in a general election or a by-election
- Have at least three officers, in addition to the party leader, who live in Canada and are eligible to vote
- Have an auditor
- Submit a copy of the party's resolution appointing its leader
- Have an agent who is qualified to sign contracts
- Submit a letter stating that the party will support one or more of its members as candidates for election

3. The party's name, abbreviation, or logo (if any) must not resemble those of any other party and must not include the word "independent." Once the Chief Electoral Officer has verified the party's application (confirming that 250 electors are members of the party and that the party has met all the other requirements), and is satisfied that the party's name and logo will not be confused with those of another registered or eligible party, he or she will inform the party leader that the party is eligible for registration.

Source: Elections Canada

Green Party Leaders

The Green Party is one of Canada's younger federal political parties. As a result, it has less of a historical base than some of the other Canadian political parties. Party leaders have worked hard to get the message of the Green Party into Canada's political mainstream. They have made serious inroads that have increased their public visibility on a national level.

Green Party Leaders

NAME	TERM
Trevor Hancock	1983–1984
Seymour Trieger	1984–1988
Kathryn Cholette	1988–1990
Chris Lea	1990–1996
Wendy Priesnitz	1996–1997
Harry Garfinkle	1997
Joan Russow	1997–2001
Chris Bradshaw	2001–2003
Jim Harris	2003–2006
Elizabeth May	2006–

FIRST PARTY LEADER
TREVOR HANCOCK
1948–

Dr. Trevor Hancock was born in England in 1948. After immigrating to Canada, he practised as a family doctor before continuing his studies in public health at the University of Toronto. He has become a well-known consultant on health promotion, sustainable development, and healthy cities, having worked with the World Health Organization and a variety of international public health organizations. He became the first leader of the Green Party of Canada in 1983 and was one of 60 Green Party candidates who ran in the 1984 election.

Trevor Hancock became a family physician after completing his medical program in Great Britain.

FOURTH PARTY LEADER
CHRIS LEA

Chris Lea was the longest-serving leader of the Green Party to date. In the 1990s, Green Party leaders were figureheads only. The party made all major decisions as a group. Lea tried to take a larger role. During his tenure, the first comprehensive Green Party policy document was distributed electronically. In the 1993 election, he was the first Green leader to make a national tour. A professional designer, he also created the first Green Party logo. He was a candidate for a Toronto **riding** in both the 1993 federal election and 1995 provincial election.

SIXTH LEADER
JOAN RUSSOW
1938–

Joan Russow is an environmentalist from Victoria, British Columbia. Under her leadership, the Green Party broadened its platform to include social issues as well as environmental issues. This linked the natural environment to a wide range of global human rights issues such as poverty, health care, and **globalization**. Russow resigned from the party in 2001. Since then, she has criticized the Green Party for moving away from its basic principles.

Russow received a Ph.D. in interdisciplinary studies from the University of Victoria.

JIM HARRIS
1961–

Jim Harris has been active in politics since the 1980s. Originally a Progressive Conservative, he joined the Green Party in the late 1980s. He was instrumental in organizing the Ontario Green Party's 1990 election campaign and became leader of the federal Green Party in 2003. Harris is a well-known Canadian author, having written bestsellers such as *The 100 Best Companies to Work for in Canada* and *The Learning Paradox*.

Association Magazine has ranked Harris as one of Canada's top 10 speakers.

EIGHTH LEADER

ELIZABETH MAY
1954–

Elizabeth May became leader of the Green Party in 2006 after a celebrated career as an environmental activist, author, and lawyer. She was born in the U.S. state of Connecticut in 1954, but moved to Nova Scotia as a teenager. She has been involved in various anti-nuclear and environmental protests, including a protest to prevent the spraying of pesticides on Nova Scotia's forests. In 2001, she went on a 17-day hunger strike to protest inaction over the clean-up of the Sydney tar ponds. After graduating from Dalhousie Law School in 1983, she worked briefly as a policy adviser to the Minister of Environment in the Conservative government.

Elizabeth May was the executive director of the Sierra Club of Canada from 1989 to 2006. The Sierra Club campaigns for environmental awareness.

🍁 People who supported the counter-culture of the 1960s experimented with alternative lifestyles. Some formed communes in which they grew their own food and lived off the land.

International Roots, 1960–2001

The global green movement began in response to issues and principles that fuelled the **counter-culture** of the 1960s. In that decade, young people around the world rejected the concept of consumer culture, which encouraged mass consumption and continuous economic growth regardless of their effects on workers and the environment. Instead, they promoted the values of peace, social justice, and ecological harmony that have become the basis of green policy worldwide.

At first, environmentalists worked at the **grass roots** level in community organizations and small businesses that promoted such things as healthy foods, organic farming, and renewable energy sources. Later, these small groups joined together in coalitions to work more effectively on a provincial or national scale to promote environmental concerns, non-violence, and social justice. Seeing the need for political action, Green parties were formed to urge national governments to make the political reforms

necessary to put these values into practice. What has become a global political movement in the 21st century began in New Zealand in 1972 when the Values Party was formed. The Values Party was the first national political environmentalist party in the world. Other countries followed suit, and in 1983, the first Green Party politicians were elected to national office in West Germany.

During the 1990s, Green parties from around the world met and formed a committee to create a network through which they could exchange news. In April 2001, the Global Green Network was officially created at a meeting in Canberra, Australia, and 800 Greens from 72 countries approved the first ever Charter of the Global Greens. In 2011, there were more than 100 Green parties worldwide, with elected politicians in Canada, Mexico, Australia, New Zealand, and many European countries.

In 2011, there were more than 100 Green parties worldwide.

IS GLOBAL WARMING NATURAL OR HUMANMADE?

Greenhouse gases (GHGs) in Earth's atmosphere trap heat from the Sun, causing the temperature on Earth to rise. This contributes to **global warming**. There has been debate as to whether natural or humanmade gases are causing this climate change.

NATURAL | HUMANMADE

Earth has gone through a series of cooling and warming cycles over the course of its history. Natural increases in water vapour in the Earth's atmosphere caused by changes in solar activity and natural phenomena, such as volcanic eruptions, are responsible for the current warming trend.

Temperature changes in the past century are too extreme to be explained by natural causes. Greenhouse gases, particularly carbon dioxide, produced from the burning of **fossil fuels** have caused the temperature to rise at an accelerated rate.

THE RESULT

Today, scientists and organizations on both sides claim to have evidence to support their cause. Some people have even suggested that global warming is not real.

Global Green Network

Green parties from countries on each continent belong to federations that together form the Global Green Network.

1. African Greens Federation (26 member countries)
2. Federation of Green Parties of the Americas (13 member countries)
3. Asia-Pacific Green Network (11 member countries)
4. European Green Party (35 member countries)
5. Seven other countries have observer status with the organization.

Jeanette Fitzsimons was the co-leader of the New Zealand Green Party from 1995 to 2009. She represented the party in Parliament until 2010.

Stephane Pocrain was the national spokesperson for the French Green Party. In 2006, he ran for the French presidency.

Colombia's Green Party made effective use of the Internet during the 2010 election campaign. They held web chats and online press conferences to get their message out to the public. The party placed second in the election.

The Early Years, 1978–2001

The first Green party in the western hemisphere was formed in Canada in the late 1970s to oppose the building of a nuclear power plant in the Maritimes. It was called the "Small Party"—a reference to E.F. Schumacher's economics book, *Small is Beautiful*, which was published in 1973. The party fielded 11 candidates in the 1980 federal election. None were successful, but the party gained media attention for environmental issues.

In 1983, some of the candidates went on to found the Green Party of Canada. Campaigning on the established Green principles, 60 Green Party candidates ran in the 1984 federal election under the leadership of Dr. Trevor Hancock.

The party earned only 0.21 percent of the popular vote, which was not enough to secure election funding from the federal government. However, over the next few years, the party developed its organization and increased its membership. It ran 79 candidates in the 1993 federal election.

Joan Russow, an academic and environmental activist, became leader of the Green Party in 1997, just before a federal general election was called. Russow was not elected, but under her leadership, the party continued to expand its policies regarding human rights and peace issues. She resigned from the Green Party in 2001 and was replaced by Chris Bradshaw on an interim basis.

> Over the next few years, the party developed its organization and increased its membership.

🍁 Elizabeth May was one of the founding members of the Small Party.

SHOULD CANADA INCREASE ITS USE OF NUCLEAR POWER?

Nuclear power plants generate electricity from **radioactive** elements such as uranium and plutonium. The "Small Party" was formed by anti-nuclear activists, but pro-nuclear supporters claim that nuclear power is environmentally friendly. Which side is most convincing?

PRO

Nuclear plants generate enormous amounts of electricity while producing very low greenhouse gas emissions. They therefore have a minimal effect on global warming and do not expose people to air pollution. Nuclear plants do not require a supply of non-renewable fossil fuels. The technology is already developed and has many mechanisms in place to prevent accidents.

ANTI

Nuclear plants produce enormous amounts of radioactive waste. This waste can take thousands of years to become inert and can be used to produce nuclear weapons. Even a small accident at the plant can have catastrophic results. This risk will increase if more nuclear plants are built, especially if they become a target of terrorist attacks.

THE RESULT

Nuclear power has been out of favour with governments and the public alike, owing to dangers and difficulties in storing radioactive waste, accidents, and the cost and delays in refurbishing older reactors.

Provincial Green parties were growing alongside the federal party. By 2001, six provinces had their own Green parties.

1. The British Columbia party started in 1983.
2. The Ontario party was created in 1983.
3. The Green Party of Alberta was founded in 1986.
4. The Green parties of Saskatchewan and Manitoba were created in 1998.
5. Quebec created its Green Party in 1985. It did not run candidates in the 1998 election and lost its party status. It regrouped in 2001.

Jane Sterk was the leader of the B.C. Green Party during the 2009 provincial election. The party placed third in the polls, but received only 8.21 percent of the popular vote.

Scott McKay was elected the leader of Quebec's Green Party in 2007. However, he lost the leadership in 2008 following the party's poor showing in the provincial election.

Election Breakthroughs, 2004–2006

The party now qualified for federal subsidies that allowed it to expand and raise its profile nationally.

Jim Harris, an author and speaker on leadership, became leader of the national party in 2003 after serving for almost two years as president of the Green Party of Ontario. Under Harris's leadership, the Green Party of Canada increased its share of the popular vote, but suffered internal divisions over management of the party and its finances.

Harris was, however, able to improve the party's national standings. The 2004 federal election was a historic moment for the Green Party. First, the party was only the fourth federal political party to run a candidate in every federal riding. This demonstrated that the Green Party was truly national, with support across the country. Secondly, although none of the Green Party candidates were elected, the party gained 4.3 percent of the popular

vote. The party now qualified for federal **subsidies** that allowed it to expand and raise its profile nationally.

The party again ran a full slate of candidates in the 2006 election. Despite optimism that the party would get a million votes, it made only a small gain over 2004, receiving 4.5 percent of the popular vote.

Following the 2006 election, Harris decided that he would not stand for re-election. He was succeeded as leader by Elizabeth May. In a by-election held in London, Ontario, that year, May finished second to the Liberal candidate. This was the best-ever result for a Green Party candidate. May beat out the Conservative and NDP candidates, with 25.8 percent of the vote.

THE GREEN PARTY LEFT- OR RIGHT-WING?

The ideology, or belief system, of a political party is usually described by placing it on the **political spectrum** between **fascism** on the far right and **communism** on the far left. Parties on the left are perceived to support the rights of the people, while parties on the right are perceived to support the rights of the individual. Canada's Conservative Party is right of centre, the Liberals left of centre, and the NDP on the left. The ideology of the Green Party is harder to place.

LEFT ## RIGHT

Those who argue the Green Party is left-wing point to policies such as its belief that government must provide social services for the unemployed, low-income families, minorities, and the disadvantaged. The party also opposes **private sector** involvement in health care or education.

People who believe the Green Party is right-wing note that the party believes government must strengthen the economy and manage finances. The tax reduction policies proposed as part of the 2004 Green Tax Shift were labelled 'eco-capitalist' and associated with the political right.

THE RESULT

The Green Party believes in taking a **non-partisan** approach that adopts good ideas wherever they originate. Adopting strategies from both the right and the left makes Green policies attractive to voters from across the spectrum. However, this support is dispersed all over the country, and other parties have adopted some of the Green proposals. As a result, this approach has not led to electoral success.

Starting in 2004, the Green Party became known for its innovative use of electronic media.

1. During the 2004 election, it used **wiki** technology to create its "Living Platform." The program allowed party members and supporters to participate in deciding the party's election platform.
2. "Green Bloggers" was created to support the Green Party of Canada. The group has grown to include environmental bloggers from other countries.
3. The party uses social networking media, such as Twitter and Facebook, to communicate ideas to the public and create a sense of community.

The Green Party has more than 10,000 followers on Twitter.

Facebook has allowed the Green Party to communicate directly with its supporters and to hear their views on various topics. This has allowed the party to shape its platform.

Climate Planning, 2007

Under May's leadership, the party began a campaign for visibility within the country. On June 5, 2007, Elizabeth May released the *Green Party Climate Plan: A New Energy Revolution to Avert Global Catastrophe*. The plan proposed a series of measures that would create a **low-carbon economy**. The measures included encouraging the use of renewable energy sources, increasing energy efficiency, and encouraging environmentally-friendly practices. The Green Party claimed that, by implementing these measures, Canada would thrive economically, reduce its greenhouse emissions, and take on a leadership role in the global campaign for climate control.

The plan is controversial in proposing a **carbon tax** on greenhouse gas emissions. Industries would be taxed on every tonne of carbon dioxide they produce. The revenue from this would be used to give tax reductions to individuals and businesses that eliminate or produce less greenhouse gases. This **carbon tax shift** would increase the cost of gasoline for everybody, but the plan suggests that revenue could be used to encourage industries that rely on fossil fuels to invest instead in cleaner energy sources.

The plan also included a **cap-and-trade market** for the big emitters of carbon dioxide, such as mining, oil, gas, and electricity companies who are responsible for about half of Canada's total emissions. In this scheme, the government sets a cap, or limit, on the amount of a pollutant a company is permitted to produce. If the company wishes to exceed that cap, it must purchase emission permits from other companies who need fewer. In this way, industries are encouraged to reduce pollution.

On June 5, 2007, Elizabeth May released the Green Party Climate Plan.

❦ The Green Party supports renewable energy projects such as wind farms. A single wind turbine can produce enough electricity to power 500 homes for a year.

HONOURING THE KYOTO PROTOCOL

The Kyoto Protocol is an international agreement signed in December 1997 in Kyoto, Japan, that went into effect in February 2005. Its goal is to reduce worldwide greenhouse gas emissions. Canada agreed to reduce emissions to 6 percent below 1990 levels by 2012. Its success in achieving this goal has been hampered, however, from differing perspectives on the issue.

YES

The Greens, Liberals, and NDP all favour reducing GHG emissions to address the effects of global warming. They believe that reducing emissions will benefit the economy by forcing industries to be more energy efficient and by stimulating the development of new technologies. This will create jobs and encourage individuals to improve energy efficiency in their homes, as well as take advantage of environmentally-friendly public transit.

NO

The Conservatives, business groups, and fossil fuels industries are generally against the Kyoto Protocol, arguing that it will ruin the economy and eliminate jobs. The United States withdrew from the protocol in 2001, deciding to implement a plan of its own that would not hurt its economy. If Canadian companies have to invest money in reducing emissions, they will be unable to compete against American industries that are operating to different standards.

THE RESULT

Canada's emissions have increased by 24 to 30 percent above the 1990 level since the Kyoto Protocol was signed. Currently, the Conservative government does not intend to live up to Canada's promised reductions. It argues that until the U.S. and emerging major GHG producers such as China and India have to make reductions too, it is pointless for Canada to take action.

The Green Party Climate Plan made other suggestions to create a greener Canada.

1. The Greens wanted to launch a plan for Canada's Green Century, with a commitment to make Canada one of the most energy-efficient, sustainably powered nations in the world.
2. They recommended that all federal buildings be **retrofit** to a high level of efficiency by 2025 and that funding be provided for energy retrofits to museums, universities, schools, and hospitals.
3. They suggested that walking, cycling, transit, coaches, rail, and video conferencing be strongly supported by the government.

Solar energy is a renewable and clean form of energy. Unlike other energy sources, it does not burn oil and its creation does not produce toxic waste.

Retrofitting is the process of updating older buildings to make them energy efficient.

Vision Green details the strategies and goals of the Green Party.

Vision Green, 2007

Through *Vision Green*, the Green Party wanted to show how it was different from other Canadian political parties.

To further engage the country in the Green Party's platform and prepare for a possible election, the party published a comprehensive policy document called *Vision Green* in 2007. It had been prepared in consultation with experts and grass roots participants in a series of workshops held across Canada.

In *Vision Green*, the party proposed a reduction of emissions to 30 percent below 1990 levels by 2020 and an 80 percent reduction by 2040. Besides reducing carbon dioxide emissions by industry, the Green Party proposed encouraging individuals and small businesses to protect the environment through more efficient use of resources such as public transit, non-polluting vehicles, energy efficient buildings, promoting alternative energy, and raising public awareness of the need to conserve and re-use resources. Other environmental policies included provisions to preserve and restore air and water quality, protect the Arctic, expand Canada's national parks, and protect endangered species.

Vision Green included non-environmental policies as well. Social programs, foreign policy, and its vision for governing Canada and Canadians was described in depth in various sections of the report. Through *Vision Green*, the Green Party wanted to show how it was different from other Canadian political parties.

A REAL POLITICAL PARTY?

Some people believe that the Green Party is just the political wing of the environmentalist movement in Canada. Hence, the Greens have been accused of being a radical, one-issue party that cannot hope to win power and would not know how to rule if it did. Is the Green Party a real political party?

YES

Vision Green is a comprehensive platform document outlining policies on all the major issues facing Canadians, including aboriginal government, health care, education, and military and foreign policy. The party claims its policies are designed to be "cost-effective, deliver results, and benefit people, the economy, and the environment."

NO

The vast majority of Green candidates have no experience in politics and no chance of winning an election. Until Jim Harris took over, the party lacked organization and structure, and its policies were left-leaning and **utopian**. Under Elizabeth May's leadership, the party has risked losing votes through taking a non-partisan approach and seeming to advocate **strategic voting**.

THE RESULT

The Green Party has responded to criticisms by providing detailed policies and putting a **shadow cabinet** in place to comment on government initiatives between elections.

In Vision Green, the Green Party of Canada identified four major threats to society.
1. The climate crisis
2. Economic instability
3. Increasing **militarism**
4. A growing gap between the rich and the poor

Global warming will impact negatively on animals that rely on a cold climate for their survival. The world's polar bear population is already being affected as a result of global warming.

Factories and power plants send greenhouse gases into the atmosphere. These gases play a role in global warming.

Many countries, including North and South Korea, use their military strength as a way to resolve problems.

A Step Forward, 2008

The Greens had high hopes that, with their popular new leader and increased public concern about global warming, they would elect several representatives in the October 2008 election. May declared her intention to improve the quality of debate in the campaign by focusing on the issues and being non-partisan.

The Green Party's growth in the previous election provided it with more funding for its 2008 campaign. However, it still did not operate on the type of budget Canada's major parties did. May's decision to tour the country on environmentally-friendly VIA Rail therefore made financial as well as ideological sense. With the extra funding, the party was able to use television advertising, employ extra staff, and develop an electronic voter-identification program.

The additional funds helped the Green Party communicate its message to a larger audience and improve its national standing. In the election, the Green Party again increased its share of the popular vote, this time to 6.8 percent. May's highly publicized attempt to unseat Peter MacKay, the Conservative Minister of National Defence, was, however, unsuccessful. She came second to MacKay, receiving 32 percent of the vote in contrast to his 47 percent. This result was repeated in ridings across the country. Once again, the Green Party had failed to elect a single member to Parliament.

> **The Greens had high hopes that, with their popular new leader and increased public concern about global warming, they would elect several representatives.**

❧ Elizabeth May's VIA Rail tour took her from one end of the country to the other, with several stops along the way.

PROPORTIONAL REPRESENTATION

Canada currently uses the majority election system in which one MP is elected per constituency. In a proportional representation system, seats are assigned according to the number of votes each party receives. Most of the world's leading democracies already use proportional representation. Should Canada follow suit?

YES

The current system does not translate the popular vote into seats, leaving many voters feeling their views are not represented and their votes do not count. Proportional representation would be fairer and more democratic, reflect the diversity of opinion and ethnicity in Canada, and encourage higher voter turnout at the polls. It would force parties to compromise and build consensus.

NO

Proportional representation tends to produce short-lived minority or coalition governments that can be weak and indecisive. It gives minority parties too much power and enables undesirable extremist parties to gain representation. In Canada's current system, MPs serve the constituency they campaign in and are therefore more involved in local issues.

THE RESULT

The 2008 election illustrates why the Greens and others support electoral reform. The Green Party earned nearly one million votes across the country, but did not elect a single MP. In contrast, the Bloc Québécois received 1.3 million votes but elected 50 MPs. It was also the lowest voter turnout ever for a federal election.

Key Issues 2008 of Election

Several issues came to the forefront during the 2008 election.
1. The Conservative government's poor economic planning.
2. The Conservative's failure to live up to Canada's Kyoto Protocol commitment.
3. Mayors of Canada's major cities demanded more federal funding for infrastructure repairs.
4. The Conservative's proposed cuts to arts and culture groups.

The funding cuts proposed by the Harper government were going to affect international marketing of Canadian arts groups, including the National Ballet of Canada.

In 1998, the Liberal government made a commitment to reduce Canada's gas emissions 6 percent by 2012.

The Canadian automotive industry is a major contributor to the country's economy. In recent years, the federal government has supplied the industry with about $250 million to develop more fuel-efficient and eco-friendly vehicles.

Expanding Policies, 2009–2011

As the Green Party has gained national recognition, it has begun to develop policies outside of its green mandate. These policies are meant to indicate the party's ability to govern the country. Therefore, they cover issues such as the economy, minorities, health care, and foreign policy.

In 2009, the party published its economic stimulus package. The package set out a series of measures that would help foster economic growth while maintaining the party's environmentalist approach. For instance, as a result of the worldwide economic downturn, thousands of workers in traditional industries, such as automobile manufacturing, lost their jobs. Instead of giving these industries funding to preserve jobs, the Green Party proposed creating new jobs by investing money in smaller businesses and local projects and programs based on green principles.

The Green Party's commitment to gender equality was demonstrated in 2009 when members passed a resolution to establish a Women's Council to encourage the participation of women within the Party. Other policies have been developed to show support for Canada's Aboriginal Peoples as well.

With an expanding policy base and its increased visibility, the Green Party is gaining credibility with the electorate. It has also achieved credibility within the political environment. Several Green Party policies have been adopted by the Liberals and NDP, indicating that the Greens have forced other parties to develop environmental policies. This growing credibility became even more apparent in 2011 when Elizabeth May became the first member of the Green Party of Canada to be elected to the House of Commons.

With an expanding policy base and its increased visibility, the Green Party is gaining credibility with the electorate.

SHOULD CORPORATE TAXES BE CUT?

In 2008, the Conservative government began a program of yearly reductions in corporate taxes from 19.5 percent in 2008 to 15 percent in 2012. Critics asked whether this was the right strategy.

YES

The Conservative Party, business leaders, and business organizations claimed that cuts to business taxes benefitted the economy by making more money available for growth and investment and creating more jobs. They claimed that high business taxes made Canadian products more expensive and therefore less attractive to Canadian or foreign buyers.

NO

green
PARTY OF CANADA

The Green Party and Liberals agreed that business taxes should not be decreased. Critics argued that corporate tax cuts are the least effective job creation measure, have little impact on encouraging investments, and require the government to borrow money to finance them. They also benefit companies that are already doing well, rather than companies that need the most help.

THE RESULT

Although good talking points for politicians, tax cuts are only one factor determining the course of the economy. Canada's recovery was relatively successful compared to other countries. After July 2009, unemployment decreased, exports and imports increased, and the Canadian dollar gained value. On the other hand, inflation increased, and the national debt surpassed its 1996–1997 peak of $563 billion.

The Women's Council was created with four main objectives.

1. To promote the nomination and election of Green Party women to Parliament
2. To strive for gender equity by seeking, encouraging, and supporting women to run for office within the Green Party of Canada
3. To establish a Women's Club in each electoral district
4. To further develop the structural and administrative functions of the Women's Council

Adriane Carr was a founding member of British Columbia's Green Party and served as its first leader. She is now a deputy leader with the federal Green Party.

Kate Storey serves as the Green Party's agriculture critic. She practises organic farming in her home province of Manitoba.

TIMELINE

The green movement has been gaining ground worldwide since the 1960s. Canada joined the movement early, and the movement has been growing ever since. The creation of the Green Party has brought environmental issues to the forefront of Canadian politics and society. This timeline indicates some of the national and international steps taken in the move toward sustainability.

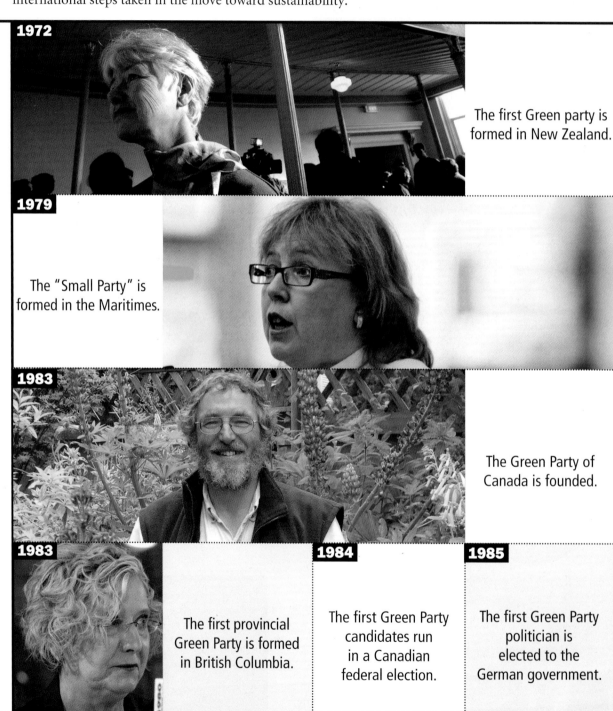

1972

The first Green party is formed in New Zealand.

1979

The "Small Party" is formed in the Maritimes.

1983

The Green Party of Canada is founded.

1983

The first provincial Green Party is formed in British Columbia.

1984

The first Green Party candidates run in a Canadian federal election.

1985

The first Green Party politician is elected to the German government.

1988

The Kyoto Protocol is signed.

1999

Art Vanden Berg becomes the first Canadian Green to be elected to municipal office.

2001

The Charter of Global Greens is signed.

2004

The Green Party of Canada runs a full slate of candidates in the federal election and qualifies for federal subsidies.

2006

Elizabeth May becomes leader of the Green Party of Canada.

2007

Vision Green is published.

2008

Elizabeth May participates in the televised leaders' debate.

2009

The Green Party of Canada's Women's Council is established.

2010

The Green Party of Canada votes to keep Elizabeth May as leader until after the next election.

2011

Elizabeth May is elected to the House of Commons.

10 FAST FACTS
ABOUT THE GREEN PARTY

2 In 1998, the party forbade membership in any other federal political party. This was intended to prevent the party from being taken over.

1 Under Elizabeth May, the Green Party won 3.9 percent of the national vote in the 2011 federal election.

3 Founded in 2006, the Young Greens is the youth arm of the Green Party of Canada. The group is open to members between the ages of 14 and 29.

4 In 2008, independent MP Blair Wilson joined the party, becoming its first member of Parliament. He was defeated in the next election before he had a chance to sit as a Green MP.

5 Prior to 2008, the Green Party had been excluded from televised election debates because it had no sitting members of Parliament. This changed when Blair Wilson joined the party. However, in the days leading up to the debate, both the Conservative and NDP leaders threatened to boycott the event if the Green Party was allowed to participate. They were forced to back down by a public outcry. At the debate, Elizabeth May surprised many viewers by effectively debating a wide range of topics, in both official languages.

6 Until the 2011 election, the Green Party was the largest of the federally registered political parties without representation in Parliament.

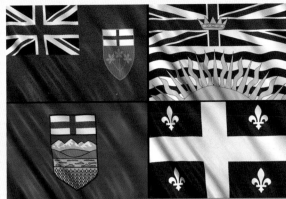

7 Most Green Party members come from the provinces of Ontario, British Columbia, Alberta, and Quebec.

green
PARTY OF CANADA

PARTI vert
DU CANADA

8 Like many other Green Parties around the world, the Green Party of Canada uses a sunflower as its logo. The sunflower represents the Sun, Earth's main source of renewable energy.

10 Besides leading the Green Party, Elizabeth May is also a student of theology. She plans to become an ordained minister in the Anglican Church.

9 In 2010, Elizabeth May was named one of the world's most influential women by *Newsweek* magazine.

WHAT IS A DEBATE?

When people debate a topic, two sides take a different viewpoint about one idea. They present logical arguments to support their views. Usually, each person or team is given a set amount of time to present its case. The presenters take turns stating their arguments until the total time set aside for the debate is used up. Sometimes, there is an audience in the room listening to the presentations. Later, the members of the audience vote for the person or team they think made the most persuasive arguments.

Debating is an important skill. It helps people to think about ideas thoughtfully and carefully. It also helps them develop rhythms of speech that others can follow easily.

Some schools have organized debating clubs as part of their after-school activities. Schools often hold debates in their history class or as part of studying about world events.

DEBATE THIS!

Every day, the news is filled with the issues facing Canada and its citizens. These issues are debated in the House of Commons and on city streets. People often have different views of these issues and support different solutions.

Following is an issue that has sparked discussion across the country. Gather your friends or classmates, and divide into two teams to debate the issue. Each team should take time to properly research the issue and develop solid arguments for their side.

One of the more controversial proposals the Green Party has developed is the idea of placing a carbon tax on greenhouse gas emissions. Industries would be taxed for their greenhouse emissions, and the revenue from the tax would go to companies that produce fewer emissions.

Are carbon taxes an appropriate way to control greenhouse gas emissions?

QUIZ

1: On what document does the Green Party base its core values?

2: Who was the first leader of the Green Party of Canada?

3: What is the Global Green Network?

4: When was the Green Party of Canada formed?

5: How was the 2004 election significant for the Green Party of Canada?

6: When was the Green Party Climate Plan released?

7: Name the four major threats to society as listed by the Green Party of Canada.

8: What is the highest number of seats the Green Party has won in a federal election?

9: What is the main purpose of the Women's Council?

10: Who was the first Green Party leader to take part in a televised leaders' debate?

Answers:
1. Charter of the Global Greens 2. Dr. Trevor Hancock 3. A network through which Green parties around the world can exchanige news 4. 1983 5. It became the fourth party to run a candidate in every federal riding, and it gained enough of the popular vote to qualify for federal funding. 6. Environment Day, June 5, 2007 7. Climate crisis, economic instability, increasing militarism, growing gap between the rich and the poor 8. One 9. To encourage the participation of women in the party 10. Elizabeth May

FURTHER RESEARCH

Suggested Reading

Harris, Jim, *Going Green*. Vancouver: Raincoast Books, 2005.

Hawkins, Howie. *Independent Politics: The Green Party Strategy Debate*. London: Haymarket Books, 2010.

May, Elizabeth. *At the Cutting Edge: The Crisis in Canada's Forests*. Toronto: Key Porter Books, 2009.

Internet Resources

Read about the Green Party of Canada directly from the source at **http://greenparty.ca**

A detailed history of the Green Party of Canada can be found at **www.thecanadianencyclopedia.com**. Just type Green Party into the search bar.

Learn more about Canada's political parties and the election process at **www.elections.ca**

GLOSSARY

biodiversity: the variability among living organisms on Earth

biosphere: the part of Earth and its atmosphere in which living organisms exist or that is capable of supporting life

cap-and-trade market: controlling pollution by providing economic incentives for achieving reduction in the emissions of pollutants

carbon tax: a tax on the emissions caused by the burning of coal, gas, and oil

carbon tax shift: a tax on carbon that increases the cost of emissions by shifting more of the tax burden to carbon-based fuels

colonies: regions ruled by a country that is usually far away

communism: a system of social organization based on the holding of all property in common, actual ownership being ascribed to the community as a whole or to the state

counter-culture: a culture with values or lifestyles in opposition to those of the establishment

democracy: a political system in which the people elect the members of their government

fascism: a system of government marked by centralization of authority under a dictator

fossil fuels: fuel sources that were created through a combination of the decomposition of plant and animal matter

globalization: the process of increasing the interdependence of the world's markets

global warming: an increase in Earth's average atmospheric temperature that causes corresponding changes in climate

grass roots: people at a local level rather than at the centre of major political activity

greenhouse gases: gases that act as a shield to trap heat in Earth's atmosphere

low-carbon economy: an economy that has a low output of greenhouse gas emissions

militarism: a policy in which military preparedness is of primary importance to a state

non-partisan: not influenced by any single political party

political spectrum: a term used to refer to the differences in ideology between the major political parties

private sector: all economic activity other than that of government

radioactive: exhibiting emission of radiation

renewable resources: any natural resources that can be replenished naturally with the passage of time

responsible government: a form of government in which decisions cannot become law without the support of the majority of elected representatives

retrofit: to provide something with parts, devices, or equipment not available at the time of original manufacture

riding: an electoral district

shadow cabinet: members of the opposition party who function as unofficial counterparts to the cabinet ministers of the party in power

social justice: fair and proper administration of laws conforming to the natural law that all persons, irrespective of ethnic origin, gender, possessions, race, and religion, are to be treated equally and without prejudice

strategic voting: voting for a candidate or party other than one's first choice in the hopes of preventing another candidate from winning an election

subsidies: financial aid given by the government to individuals or groups

utopian: idealized perfection

wiki: a piece of server software that allows users to freely create and edit Web page content using any Web browser

INDEX